Preface

My introduction to deacon Ministry was unfortunately an unpleasant event. I had just committed my life to pastoral ministries. My pastor invited me to attend a 4 night training course on ministry of the deacon. On the third evening a conflict over nursery policies erupted. The week-long study lost its meaning, the deacons failed to respond , and by the time the dust had cleared 3 active deacons, one future pastor, and several family members left the church.

I quickly learned the value of deacon training and the importance of pastors and deacons working together. I vowed that I would devote myself to learning all I could about deacons and their ministry. After many hours of research I wrote a simple study guide, and taught the principles of deacon ministry to my whole church. The success of the teaching caught the eye of my director of missions, then state workers and even some at the national convention. For the next 20 years deacon ministry would be at the center of my life's work.

Through the years I have been encouraged by numerous people to keep working in deacon ministry. One such man, Ceasar Gonzales, a Southern California Hispanic deacon contributed in both, words and finances to make this work a reality. Ray and Susan McBride of Lake Village Arkansas also made a generous contribution to allow for the completion of this writing. I am deeply indebted (spiritually) to both of these families who trusted my efforts.

The real reason for writing this small book is to encourage deacons to keep up the Lord's work. The importance of this book is not centered on who I am, but on the lives of deacons everywhere who love their pastors, their churches, and their Lord.

May God bless them all.

Tom

Table Of Contents

Parakaleo: The Heart of Deacon Ministry

by Tom Stringfellow with Jim L. Wilson

1

The Pay is "Out of This World!"

How Much Does a Deacon get paid?

During the spring of 1997, I conducted a Deacon Training Retreat for a church six hours north of my home. Since my wife was unable to attend, my twelve-year-old grandson agreed to accompany me. I was proud to have my "assistant" along who helped by passing out materials and collecting registration cards.

During the drive, he turned our conversation to details of the conference. I explained what we would do and what he could expect. He surprised me with his next question, "Grandpa, are they paying you anything?" He wanted all the facts, including the amount, travel expense reimbursements, and finally who was willing to pay for my efforts.

Amazed by his curiosity, I explained that some money came from our denomination, some from the host church, and some from the deacons themselves. He shrieked, "Do you mean that deacons are paying you to tell them how to do their work in the church?" After a short period of silence, he asked another question, "How much do the deacons get paid?" When I told him they are volunteers, he couldn't believe that men who served without pay, would pay me to train them!

During the quiet moments that followed our conversation,

I thought about the rewards of deacon ministry. My mind raced to events from twenty years before--I thought about Bobby's hands.

Bobby's Hands

Bobby's whole family was a valuable part of our congregation. His father, Dan, was a Navy Submarine Officer and served as a part of our deacon ministry. Anne, his mother, did a lot of everything else; teaching, cooking, singing, and caring for families.

The couple, for the early years of marriage, thought that they could not have children. Like Sarah and Abraham, God filled their home with laughter when He gave them a son. Then the next year, God gave them another son, another year and another son. It finally came to a halt when the fourth son, Bobby, entered the world. Four in a row, all beautiful, healthy, and each one a carbon copy of the others.

In August 1977, Dan left for a ninety-day submarine cruise. He would not see sunlight, or have any contact with his family until he returned. With her husband away, Anne volunteered to serve as nurse and cook for our associational youth camp. Their neighbor on the Navy base volunteered to care for Dan and Anne's four boys, so Anne could go. The arrangements looked perfect. Anne had a good relationship with her neighbor and completely trusted her. She recently joined our church after Anne led her to the Lord.

Wednesday night after dinner, the children began to help with the clean up chores. With six children aged five and under, this was no small task. Doug, Bobby's two and a half year-old brother, led Bobby to the bathroom of the duplex side occupied by the neighbor. What Doug did not know was

2

the plumbing in this side of the duplex was the reverse of his own. He turned the only bathtub faucet he could reach--the hot. Bobby fell into the scalding water, stopping his fall with outstretched arms.

The water severely burned Bobby on both hands and his lower arms. The neighbor called the military paramedics, who applied emergency care, and transported the child to the hospital at Travis Air Force Base, thirty miles away. While in route, the hospital assembled a specialist medical team to care for Bobby.

They called me as the ambulance was pulling away. I immediately called Gary Cowan, the deacon assigned to minister to this family, and we left for the hospital.

We had a hard time finding Bobby. First he went to the emergency room, then to the operating room. We caught up with him at the Pediatric Intensive Care Unit around 11:00 p.m. They suspended his arms above his head, and tied his body to the bottom and sides of the bed to eliminate the possibility of excessive movement. Bobby was heavily sedated but still thrashed as he slept.

Bobby awoke the first time around midnight. His eyes darted around the room until they fixed on his pastor and deacon. Finally, after nearly seven hours of torture at the hands of strangers, he saw some familiar faces. It was a small, delicate, and somewhat unsure, but unmistakable--Bobby smiled. He drifted back into a peaceful sleep.

Around one in the morning, the burn specialist joined us for a few moments to relate the seriousness of his injuries. He said that Bobby could experience full recovery, or more likely, the limited use of his hands for the rest of his life. Regardless, he would require treatment for many years. After a time of prayer, we returned home.

The deacons' wives jumped into action and responded to the family's needs. The church prepared meals, arranged for baby sitting, did the laundry, and cleaned their house.

Dan returned from the sea a few weeks later. He and Anne prayed and worked diligently at helping the traumatized children recover from their ordeal. They continued Bobby's treatment at Travis Hospital for the remaining year of Dan's assignment on Mare Island. The next summer, they moved to their next duty station on the East Coast.

We never lost touch with this family. We exchanged cards and letters with them during the years that followed. Often they would include an update on Bobby's progress.

Twelve years later, they came through town again and visited our church. They spent Saturday night on the church parking lot in their camper.

Sunday morning, Gary and I arrived at the church around 7:00 a.m. to turn on the heaters, prepare the rooms for the activities of the day, and make coffee for the early arrivers. Around 9:00 a.m. the doors to the fellowship hall opened with a loud clatter, in walked a gangly-looking teenager, tripping into the room. We watched from the other end of the room as he stretched out his discolored hands in our direction. He said, "I want you to see my hands."

Bobby moved rapidly toward us as we stood and exchanged tearful hugs. He thanked us repeatedly for being with him and the rest of the family during their time of need. He then said, "I know I was too young to remember the two of you at my bedside, in fact I don't remember the burn or even being in the hospital. But I know all about what happened and what you did for us. I have heard my parents'

4

testimony many times through the years. They have shared what happened to us in every Sunday School class and every church testimony service for as long as I can remember."

Bobby is a student at Liberty University preparing to follow God's call into youth ministries. His mother describes him as ". . . a stalwart Christian young man who displays a consistent level of maturity both socially and spiritually." His hands show only minor scarring, and though sensitive to cold and heat, are fully functional. The rest of the family continues in faithfulness to Christ. It was a joy to "come beside" Bobby and his family during their time of need.

In Matthew 25:31-46, Jesus reminds us of the promise of eternal rewards for those found worthy. Verses thirty-four through forty read:

"Then the King will say to those on His right, 'come you who are blessed by my Father; take your inheritance, the kingdom prepared for you since the creation of the world. For I was hungry and you gave me something to eat, I was thirsty and you gave me something to drink, I was a stranger and you invited me in, I needed clothes and you clothed me, I was sick and you looked after me, I was in prison and you came to visit me. Then the righteous will answer him, Lord, when did we see you hungry and feed you, or thirsty and give you something to drink? When did we see you a stranger and invite you in, or needing clothes and clothe you? When did we see you sick or in prison and go to visit you? The King will reply, 'I tell you the truth, whatever you did for one of the least of these brothers of mine, you did it for me.'"

Could there ever be a greater reward than what awaits us in eternity? God pays deacons, but not with money. The reward for faithful service is far beyond anything that money can buy. Unlike money or power, it lasts for eternity.

Gary and I will never forget Bobby's hands.

2

 ## What is the Deacons' "Business?"

Reestablishing the Foundation

Acts 6:1-7 KJV And in those days, when the number of the disciples was multiplied, there arose a murmuring of the Grecians against the Hebrews, because their widows were neglected in the daily ministration. [2] Then the twelve called the multitude of the disciples unto them, and said, It is not reason that we should leave the word of God, and serve tables. [3] Wherefore, brethren, look ye out among you seven men of honest report, full of the Holy Ghost and wisdom, whom we may appoint over this business. [4] But we will give ourselves continually to prayer, and to the ministry of the word.   [5] And the saying pleased the whole multitude: and they chose Stephen, a man full of faith and of the Holy Ghost, and Philip, and Prochorus, and Nicanor, and Timon, and Parmenas, and Nicolas a proselyte of Antioch: [6] Whom they set before the apostles: and when they had prayed, they laid their hands on them. [7] And the word of God increased; and the number of the disciples multiplied in Jerusalem greatly; and a great company of the priests were obedient to the faith.

Is Acts 6:1-7 the inauguration of deacon ministries? This passage does clearly show that the early church was growing rapidly and the Apostles needed help in maintaining their established work. This passage does not identify these new church workers as deacons. The Greek word from which we get our word deacon is only found once in the passage. Here, the translators of the Authorized Version rendered the word *diakanos* "to wait on." Specifically, the church chose these men to serve food to the Greek widows and to insure that the church did not neglect their care. While this service was necessary and valuable to the continuation of the work of the early church, it leaves many questions unanswered.

The second difficulty in interpretation comes with the understanding of the word rendered "business" (K.J.V.) or "responsibility" (N.I.V.) in verse three. R.B.C. Howell, President of the Southern Baptist Convention 1851-1859, made it clear in his book The Deaconship, that he thinks the ministry of the deacon is primarily associated with the control of finances and property management in the church, or "the business" of the church.[1]

---

[1]

Howell, R.B.C., The Deaconship, 2nd ed. (Philadelphia: Judson Press, 1946) "Every church in the first place must, in the nature of things, own more or less common property or funds, for the management of which the services of the deacons are essential." (p. 23)
"...the law enacting the Deaconship has never been repealed, changed or modified in any way. It is still in force, and if disregarded by us, we become, on that account, criminal before God. Indeed, no church, without deacons to preside

Unfortunately, he reached this conclusion because the editors of the King James Bible mistranslated the Greek word *chreia* as "business." Some concluded that the pastor cares for the spiritual needs of the flock while the deacons care for the material needs.[2]

---

over its temporal affairs, is legally or fully organized, or can properly claim to be in every respect, Christ's Church." (p. 24.)

"To devise a plan of our own, and to substitute for his, is to commit the folly of assuming to be more wise and to understand better the wants of his church than Christ himself! Remove the deacons, either by transferring them to the ministry or in another way, and the pecuniary interests of religion, always extensive and important, must revert to the clergy, be wholly neglected, or be under the control of men who have no authority in the premises. In either case the word of God is contemned, and the rights of both the church and the ministry are abused and injured. We are disobedient, presumptuous, and the blessing of God is justly forfeited. The evil is inevitable and aggravated." (p. 25)

2

Burroughs, P.E., Honoring The Deaconship, (Nashville: The Sunday School Board of the Southern Baptist Convention, 1929)

"In the division of labor and the assignment of a place to the deacon, a fairly clear line was drawn as to the relation of the deacon to the church. On one side of the line stands the

The editors of the New International Version of the Bible translated the same Greek word "responsibility," which is the correct understanding of the word. More specifically, the verse specifies the responsibilities of the seven new workers, rather than outlining the lifelong work of the generations of deacons to follow.

Biblical writers used *diakanos* to describe the life of Christ, the Apostles, the missionaries, and even the angels. A study of the word "deacon" in the New Testament reveals that the use of the word occurs more than a hundred times with a variety of translations. The primary use of the word is related to the work of the ministry. We cannot relegate it to "the business matters only."

Today, most agree that the deacon's work goes beyond the realm of business matters. In 1955, Robert Naylor introduced a new direction for deacon ministries. He felt that they were to be spiritual, not just business leaders. [3]

---

pastor. He, is shall we say, the ranking officer especially entrusted with the ministry which is more distinctly spiritual. On the other side is the deacon, standing next to the pastor, and entrusted with the care of the material interests of the church." p. 13.

[3]

Naylor, Robert, <u>The Baptist Deacon</u>, (Nashville: Broadman Press, 1955)

"It is good to select men of practical business judgment and experience as deacons. This is a minor though

Thirteen years later, Harold Foshee showed the similarity between the work of the deacon and the pastor. This was a giant step toward a vital Deacon ministry. [4] Foshee introduces the possibility of the pastor and deacons becoming partners in the ministry of the church. Though he acknowledges the possibility that some churches will continue to use deacons as business managers, he primarily encourages

---

not unimportant qualification. The chief requirements are spiritual. The deacon is a servant of the church. His life is to be matched against the needs of the members. It is certainly desirable and an advantage if he possesses a leadership ability and an effective know-how. Capable men can be spiritual men." p. 21.

[4]

Foshee, Harold The Ministry of Baptist Deacons (Nashville: Convention Press, 1968). "Deacons have served wherever their churches have assigned special work for them to do. Today's deacon does many different jobs. In some churches, deacons serve primarily in the administrative areas of finance, properties, and personnel management. In other churches, the deacons have unfortunately become boards of directors. In recent years, many church leaders have sensed the need for a nucleus of committed persons to lead churches to become dynamic witnessing and ministering fellowships. No other single group seems better qualified than the deacons to lead the crusade for spiritual renewal within the churches." (Preface)

their use as pastoral ministers. He refers to the deacons and pastors as "standing together as partners in a spiritual task. Together they serve in the pastoral ministries of a church."

Henry Webb agreed with Foshee that deacons and pastors were partners in the ministry. He believed that deacons *do* something special, and that they *are* something special. The importance of their work does not dwarf the vitality of their Christian faith.

Webb's greatest contribution is helping the deacon, deacon candidate, and the whole body of believers to recognize the deacon as an example of a true servant leader. His book Deacons: Servant Models in the Church, opens the readers minds and hearts to the inner-spirituality required for an effective ministry. According to Webb, deacons do not need to model themselves after their pastor, or other leaders, instead, their role model is Jesus Christ. [5]

5

Dr. Henry Webb. Deacons: Servant Models in the Church. (Nashville: Convention Press, 1980) "The primary model for all Christians is Jesus Christ himself. Jesus demonstrated this servant life-style throughout his ministry. The scripture makes it very clear that all believers are to pattern their lives after the Master. Certainly deacons should demonstrate the same qualities in their lives as Jesus displayed in his. The impact on grasping this concept is to return the entire understanding of the deaconship back to the very heart of Christ." p. 11, ff.

Obstacles to the Pastor--Deacon team

How do you define the relationship between the pastor and the deacons? In your church, is there a pastor--deacon team? The team concept for deacon ministries is certainly an important model for pastoral ministries. The Apostle Paul uses a metaphor of the race and the racer to describe those working in the ministry. During the Modern Olympic Games, a contingency of pacers, trainers and coaches support runners before, during, and after each event. These co-laborers serve beside their team leader at every step along the course. If the team pulls together, the runner has the opportunity to complete the course. Paul calls completion "the prize."

In Hebrews 12: 1-3, Paul reminds us that the course is not necessarily without obstacles. In the ministry race, there will always be obstacles. Pastor and deacon teams can overcome them if they train and work together. Pastors who see themselves as "superstars" not needing help will soon fail. They will soon lose the support of the rest of the team and falter. Some deacons build the obstacles rather than work as a team to overcome them. Sometimes these attitudes hold back those who are not willing to change or become a "team player."

Not long after adopting a "team approach" to doing pastoral ministries, we made home visits with each deacon. I hoped that by working with each deacon individually we could develop a consistent ministry effort with the total membership. I arranged to meet in the home of Deacon Jimmie and his family on the Naval Base where he lived and worked. We then would visit other families on the base together. Jimmie knew the plan and its content. Rather than visiting other families, he gave me a tour of the entire base, his work area, and a variety of other base features. At the end of the evening I told him that I would return to visit some of his families with him. He immediately made it clear that he had no intention of making home visits. This was a first major obstacle to an effective deacon ministry. If deacons or pastors, are unwilling to perform ministry tasks, as team members "along side" each other, the defeat of the plan is inevitable.

We cannot overemphasize the team ministry effort of pastors and deacons. The strength of the team working together will always be more successful than the combined results of those working independently.

Short-term Pastorates

One obstacle to the pastor--deacon team is short-term pastorates. According to Greg Summi, California Southern Baptist Director of Ministerial Services, California pastors change churches on the average of once every three and one half years. In 1974, the same office reported that the average pastor in California stayed a total of eighteen months. While these figures show an increase in the length of pastorates over the last twenty-three years, it obviously still reflects a serious problem--short pastorates.

When the pastor leaves a church, he leaves behind a body of deacons who become the primary leaders of the church. When this occurs three times every decade, it becomes difficult for the members to accept the next pastor coming to lead the flock. Deacons begin to see the pastor as a short-time employee of the church rather than its spiritual leader.

Many pastors never move from this short-time employee's status. Most members don't have enough time to learn to trust their new pastor before he moves to his next assignment.

Baggage

Another barrier to the pastor--deacon team is baggage from the past. When a new pastor comes to the church field, he brings the memories of his past churches and deacon bodies with him. If he had bad experiences, he may attempt to eliminate the deacons, or reduce their role.

I was a fresh new pastor accepting the unanimous call to my first full time church when I discovered there is a difference between a unanimous vote and total support. I had a lot of struggles during the first six months. I discovered resistance to almost everything I tried to start.

Six months after I arrived, the former pastor called me. His first question startled me, "Tom, are you having any trouble with the chairman of the deacons?" How did he know?

He told me that he had a special relationship with the chairman and knew that it could pose some difficulty for the next pastor. As it turned out, anytime he wanted to present a new idea, he first visited the chairman of the deacons to get his input. This conversation opened my eyes.

No wonder the deacon was opposing every idea I had, he was used to formulating these programs with the former pastor. My predecessor was more than a pastor to him; he was a co-laborer and a friend.

A couple of days later, I called the chairman of the deacons and said "Would it be possible for me to drop by Saturday morning and discuss some plans for the church?" He was very pleased to hear from me, so we made the appointment for ten-thirty Saturday. As I walked up the sidewalk to the front door, I smelled an unmistakable aroma-- homemade apple pie.

We had a pot of coffee and fresh apple pie. After discussing the plans, he let me know he opposed my proposal.

I immediately thought of something the former pastor told me a couple of days earlier, "Even if he disagrees with you, it doesn't matter, if you've gone to him before you bring it before the church." As I was getting ready to go, I suggested that we pray together and ask that God give us direction for our church and leaders. I prayed for the chairman of the deacons that God would lead him, for our church, and for the plans we were making.

When I finished, his wife spoke up, "Well I think if he's not going to tell you, I better." I thought; "Oh boy here it comes." "You know; my husband hasn't been fair to you." I said "Oh, in what way?" "Well, you know, he said a few things to criticize your leadership and he was criticizing this plan you are going to present this week." Inside, I chuckled--I knew exactly what she was talking about. She continued, "I told him to keep his mouth shut, that he had no right to criticize you because he wasn't praying for you or supporting you the way he should." I glanced his way and noticed a sheepish grin. "Yep," he said, "that's what she told me, and

I've decided to start praying for you every day that you'll be a better preacher and leader."

At the council meeting, the chairman commented on the plans, "The pastor brought this by my house last week and we talked it over. I'm not sure that I agree with the pastor, but if he's going to be our pastor, I think we ought to follow his leadership."

Several months later, during a testimony time, the chairman told this story, including how he had a different relationship with the former pastor, but that was all right with him. He said, "I was constantly criticizing our pastor until my wife rebuked me for not supporting him and praying for him. I want you all to know that I'm praying for my pastor every day. I've noticed his sermons are getting better, and he is a better leader." He sat back down, then after a brief hesitation he stood up again and said, "I just have one question, you don't think this old chairman of the deacons had a change of heart because of his prayers, do ya? You don't think it was me that was wrong." With a smile on his face, he sat back down. In his own way, he was saying, "I was critical and I was wrong, but if you want the pastor to be his best, pray for him every day."

Likewise, the deacons bring their experiences to their relationship with the new pastor. The bad experiences lead to a "they're all alike" attitude.

If he had good experiences, he may want to build strong relationships "just like in his last church." One or all of the deacons, likewise, may expect to build strong ties with the pastor and his family "just like they enjoyed the previous pastor." This, too, produces unrealistic expectations.

Are these problems insurmountable? Of course not. With the cooperation of pastor, deacons and the total church body, a "dream ministry team" is possible. The question remains; are we willing to make the required changes?

The **Parakaleo Perspective**

I believe the foundation for deacon ministries is not Acts 6:1-7; rather it is from the meaning of the Greek word "*Parakaleo*." To arrive at the heart of deacon ministries we must look beyond food service and table waiting. The mandate of the scripture goes beyond simple tasks into the deeper issues of life.

The Apostle Paul provides insight into the ministry to which God calls all Christians, the call to be a comforter and an encourager. Paul uses the word comforter or encourager **fifty-nine** times in his letters, of these, **twenty-five** occur in the first nine chapters of the book of Second Corinthians. **Ten** of those are found in chapter one, verses three to eleven.

Literally, *PARAKALEO,* means to come along side with strength or encouragement . . . to strengthen much. 2 Corinthians 1:3-11 remind us that all who receive comfort from God are to share that same comfort with others. Experience qualifies us to bring comfort to others. The ultimate calling of a Christian is to be an encourager. More specifically, all Christians are to be ministers, "coming beside" those in need. That is what the seven men did in the sixth chapter of Acts. They "came beside" the apostles to settle a conflict.

Deacons are called-out from among the church members to set the pace as comforters. They are servants of the church in meeting the needs of its members, families, and others in the community. Deacons show **PARAKALEO** so that all members can learn how to be encouragers to those in need.

When Bobby was burned, he needed someone to "come beside" him and bring comfort in his time of physical pain. His mother needed someone to "come beside" her in her time of desperate need of emotional healing.

The church did not burden deacon ministries with church business or budgets, not even with buildings or programs, but with the lives of those for whom Christ died. There are far too many Bobbys, Dans, and Annes whose church is not meeting their **PARAKALEO** needs. Qualified leaders cannot focus on less important issues when someone needs ministry. Bobby needs you; will you leave your committee meetings to go beside him?

3
Character: The Right To "Come Beside"
How Should Churches Choose Its Deacons?

Deacons serve best when selected from appropriate candidates. One of the most important factors that will determine the success or failure of your deacons' ministry is the quality of the deacon candidates. Each church must prayerfully decide its policies regarding deacon election before a selection process begins. A church without clear guidelines will soon discover a variety of misconceptions regarding this important ministry.

Some churches leave the selection process of new deacons to the pastors and deacons. Others churches allow members to nominate men from the floor in a business meeting. In some churches, a Deacon Selection Committee, consisting of deacons and others, screen the potential deacons. Sometimes the recruitment is done in secrecy, but other times it is out in the open.

Which is the best method? The one that works in your church! Because the polity and dynamics of your church may differ from the church down the street or the one across the nation, each church body must select the type of process that can work best for them.

Whom Should Churches choose for its Deacon Candidates?

Because of the delicate nature of the deacon's

responsibilities, it is imperative that the church maintains the highest possible standards for the deaconate. The apostles would only consider "men of good reputation and report" when the church chose men to wait tables. The deacon's job in the twenty-first century certainly demands a standard as high as the *table waiters* of the first century.

Before selecting anyone, take a moment to think about the skills that are necessary to do the job appropriately. These task issues relate to the actual performance of duties expected by the congregation. The church outlines the work of the deacon through the adoption of bylaw, job descriptions, or a deacon covenant. Certainly, they evaluate the candidate with biblical standards, but they should also determine if he has the other qualifications necessary to serve the church with excellence.

Some questions to consider are: Does he relate well to people? Is he a good communicator? Does he have the respect of the congregation and community? Does he have time to do the job?

Churches must make it clear to their candidates that the position of deacon carries certain energy and time demands. A candidate and the church must consider other time constraints for their existing service in the church. A deacon candidate, who also chairs a major committee, teaches Sunday School, sings in the choir, may have **all** of the qualifications for deaconate, except time. Such a candidate must consider giving up other positions if he feels that service as a deacon fulfills God's call for his life. A church that overburdens her members with excessive time demands is contributing to the possibility of its own collapse or the collapse of the family structure of those members.

Since the deaconate is a position of service, not of honor, a person in the church whose lifestyle does not allow them time to minister should not become a deacon. Though they meet the biblical qualities for deaconate, time constraints severely limit them. To select such a person would create a hardship on the individual, family members, or on the quality of the deacon's ministry.

Biblical Qualifications

The Apostle Paul gives Timothy a list of qualifications for deacons in I Timothy 3:8-12. This passage is the gold standard of Biblical material. Yet, there remains disagreement about the interpretation of the text. If you add church traditions to the scripture, it becomes even more confusing.

I Tim. 3:8-12 KJV Likewise must the deacons be grave, not doubletongued, not given to much wine, not greedy of filthy lucre; [9] Holding the mystery of the faith in a pure conscience. [10] And let these also first be proved; then let them use the office of a deacon, being found blameless. [11] Even so must their wives be grave, not slanderers, sober, faithful in all things. [12] Let the deacons be the husbands of one wife, ruling their children and their own houses well.

The key question when interpreting this text is: Was Paul

writing a list of *prescriptive* or *descriptive* qualifications? If the text is prescriptive, then verse eight teaches that he must drink wine in moderation. Since I don't drink wine, am I disqualified from serving as a deacon?

Verse twelve offers even more controversy. It teaches that he must be the husband of one wife. Is Paul referencing the cultural practice of polygamy[6], or is he forbidding [7]divorce? Can a divorced man serve as deacon? Can a single man serve as deacon? What about a widower[8], can he be a

---

[6]"Both pastors and deacons were to have only one wife (I Tim. 3:2,12). All churches agree that in his cultural setting Paul meant who were practicing polygamy, those married to more than one wife at a time, were unacceptable for these church leadership positions. What else Paul may have meant and what is appropriate for today's churches is widely disputed." (Webb, pp. 42-43)

[7]"The underlying principles is that the deacon must be right in his social and family relations. The reason must be apparent. Social and family evils affect and undo character. More, they depreciate standing and destroy influence." P.E. Burroughs, D.D., Honoring The deaconship, (The Sunday School Board of the Southern Baptist Convention, 1929) p. 30.

[8]"A misapprehension of the nature of the instructions here given has led, in various quarters to some singular errors...That a deacon shall actually have a wife...They indeed

deacon? While everyone agrees that the personal family life of the deacon must be "above reproach," we obviously do not agree on how we decide the standard of acceptability. This verse is such a lightning rod, that many churches ignore the teachings of the preceding verses and make a man's marital status the primary issue of a candidate's fitness for ministry.

I believe this is a descriptive text. Paul is describing the typical person Timothy should set aside for the deaconate. A person's marital status should not be the only deciding factor a church uses to determine a candidate's fitness for the job.

John married while very young, before he became a Christian. He was a coal miner in West Virginia who, during the depression, struggled to put food on the table. His bride grew lonely as he worked the long hours and began an affair with an old boyfriend.

He was "fit to be tied" when he discovered his wife's infidelity and filed for a divorce. Later he met a fine Christian woman who led him to faith in Jesus Christ and won his heart. He began life again with her.

Forty years later, they were still together, and serving the Lord at a Baptist Church in Arizona. Their pastor felt John was a model Christian that met the Biblical qualifications for the deaconate. The church followed their pastor's recommendation and ordained him.

---

frequently go so far as to conclude, that it disqualifies him if he has lost his wife, or if he has been married a second time! All this however, is inconsistent both with reason and the true meaning of Scripture." (Howell, p. 31)

John proved himself an asset to his congregation; he could calm a storm as quick as it began to fester. The people trusted him, listened to, and followed him.

Ordination

Are there any ordained deacons in your church that are not actively serving as deacons? Do you have some that don't even attend the worship services?

Ordination, as currently practiced, is the recognition that the individual is acting for the church for "life." This raises serious concerns when we so eagerly ordain those elected to the office of the Deaconship.

In every training event I conduct, I ask these questions. The surprising result is, with few exceptions, every church can name one or more former deacons no longer serving the Lord. Unless the church takes action to withdraw their ordination, these persons remain "ordained for life." If ordination is to have any significance, we must control it better. Churches should be as eager to withdraw ordination from those no longer participating with them as they are to ordain qualified men.

Once the church selects a candidate for ordination, they usually "set the candidate aside" for a period of time. During the "engagement" period, the deacon candidates attend meetings and minister beside the ordained deacons.

Character counts. A church should be very careful whom they ordain to this important office. Having no ordained men is better, than to have those whose lifestyle stains the high calling to "come beside" those who need him.

4

♡ **Relationships:
The Context To "Come Beside"**

Pastor John never thought it could happen to him . . . but it did. There was an organized effort to oust him from the pulpit. A small group with family ties was meeting in secret to find ways to force him out. They broke into his office and went through his things trying to find something to incriminate him. One family took new members aside to "fill them in on the pastor." They tried to "trump" up some charges and confront him in business meeting, but the word got out. That night more than a hundred supporters showed up and filled the room. The eight to ten people backed off; they knew the church was behind him. It was over . . . or was it?

It all came to a head a few months later when George called Pastor John on the phone. George stepped down as the Chairman of the Trustees right before John came to the church. He decided to spend more time traveling and less time "tied" down with church work. George's phone call made Bro. John's heart pound through his chest. "Pastor," he said, "we need to talk. Since we got back from our trip this weekend, we've had three phone calls from church members who are upset with you." He paused, "I'd like to come in with the chairman of the deacons to have a word with you."

John thought, "How could this be happening to me?" He always had a "charmed" ministry. Besides, things were going well in the church. Attendance, offerings, and baptisms were at all time highs. What was going on?

George went through a laundry list of complaints with John. The Pastor answered each of them with "the rest of the story." At the end of the meeting he said, "Pastor, it sounds like there are just some simple misunderstandings here, but I know this; if you don't change people's perceptions . . . your tenure here will be very short. You need to fix these relationship problems you are having."

In leadership, perception is everything. People's feelings or thoughts about a leader are more important than objective reality. This is what George was telling John. A leader is not successful if he has broken relationships with other leaders. Relationships are the resources pastors and deacons use to "come beside."

For deacons to "come beside" their pastor, other deacons, their congregation or the community at large, they must develop strong relationships. Unfortunately, most deacon training focuses on the tasks the deacons do and neglect the people skills necessary to minister effectively. This emphasis is disproportionate since we have centered most of the work of the church around relationships.

The work of the church and her ministers, paid or unpaid, is **people**. The only medium of effective ministries comes through the relationships with those we serve and those we work alongside. Pastor John did not have problems in his church because he wasn't a good preacher, administrator, or evangelist. His problems came because he neglected a few key relationships.

Building relationships does not occur by accident. The

building of healthy relationships requires a commitment of all involved because it takes considerable effort and time.

Do we have to wait until we have fully developed a relationship before we begin our work? Of course not. All that is necessary is that we are developing the relationship. A new pastor begins his work when he arrives on the field, but he becomes more effective as he builds relationships in the church and community.

The Seven Steps To Building Strong Relationships

Interpersonal relationships are the bonding or association that occurs between individuals or groups. Interpersonal relationships are a necessary process of human development, since God created men and women as social beings. These relationships are dynamic in nature, each having a life span of very little duration, or for a lifetime. These structures are found with varying degrees of intimacy. As dynamic entities, the intimacy level can rise or fall as it moves through its life cycle.

The lowest level of intimacy occurs in very casual or surface relationships. The highest level of intimacy occurs progressively as two people invest in, and respond to each other. The highest level of intimacy provides the highest level of personal satisfaction. When these higher levels of intimacy occur, we enhance the ability to work together effectively.

1. Initial contact:

All relationships begin with an initial meeting. This meeting may be the result of a scheduled event designed for this purpose, or by chance. Pastors and deacons may meet before the actual call of the pastor, or election of the new deacon. Individual interaction may be limited if many people are present, but this stage of the relationship provides the context for "first impressions."

2. Sharing the "here and now."

Early in the process, both sides will limit themselves to sharing the basic information about themselves. Their conversation will center on family, occupation or hobbies. The sharing normally will not reveal the inner hurts or joys of their life experiences. During this stage, they will talk about "church work" and freely exchange some ideas about their perceptions of the ministry. Their conversations will be in generalities, speaking in terms such as "deacon responsibilities are . . . " rather than using the more personal, "my responsibilities are . . . "

3. Telling life stories:

Everyone has a life story, and most are anxious to share all or part of it with anyone showing an interest. The stories that we tell in this early stage will be limited to nonthreatening issues. Most will not expose the harder struggles of life until they establish a high level of trust between the parties. As the relationship progresses, more of the deeper struggles will surface through the mutual sharing process.

4. Risking . . . making an investment:

The real growth in relationships begins when the participants risk their own standing with the group or individual by sharing a deeper truth from their life story. This may be the revelation of a personal issue not previously known. The sharing at this point moves from the surface issues to their deep feelings. Often the discussion will expose unresolved failures, pain, or struggles. This provides a giant step toward deepening the trust levels. The person initiating the risk realizes that the possibility of rejection by the other parties could close the door to further growth. Making such an investment in the process reveals a heartfelt desire to establish strong ties with the body or the individual.

5. Trust development:

The focus in the growth process is now directed toward those to whom they share the revelations in the previous step. Rejection can cause the person to withdraw from the relationship, or to internalize any future concerns rather than openly sharing them. Acceptance will establish a sense of trust. Trust provides the basis for a further deepening of the relationship.

6. Mutuality:

Mutuality occurs as the risk-taking and acceptance flows in both directions. Both sides of the relationship begin to share their feelings about past, current and future concerns. They equally accept one another. The feelings of fear in revealing failures or let downs in the exercise of faith are relieved. Those involved are more eager to seek the counsel of the other at times of hurt, loss, or difficult decisions. The wisdom or experience of one person becomes a source of strength for another. Both seek to build the esteem of the other.

7. Complete intimacy:

The final stage in the process of relationship growth

occurs when mutuality includes every issue of life. This new partnership is comfortable in calling attention to weaknesses or letdowns in the life of the other. Both operate at a full trust level. A real sense of security exists within the bounds of this relationship.

The Pastor--Deacon Relationship

The process of developing relationships is of great concern to the mutual work of the pastor, staff, and deacons. Often pastors and deacons never progress beyond steps 1, 2, or 3. Pastors and deacons need some of their relationships to progress to the final steps of development. We should not expect that every relationship will enter the final phase. No pastor or deacon should ever feel alone in the service of the Lord through the local church. Stronger relationships provide a secure foundation on which their ministry can build.

The growth of the relationship does not happen without the expenditure of time and energy of the pastors and deacons. Neglect in building relationships will negatively affect the work of both, and contribute to the early departure of the pastor as he seeks to fulfill his need for security through intimate relationships with co-laborers.

Deacon Relationships With Fellow Deacons

Deacon work often depends on two or more deacons working together on specific projects. The deacons need to resolve differences within the body as rapidly as possible. The total body of deacons must clearly define and fully agree upon their understanding of responsibilities, methods, and interactions.

Because, working in a friendly environment is more productive than working with strangers, the deacon body should plan activities that promote fellowship. Retreats, regularly scheduled dinners, or social activities, contribute greatly to the building of friendships. It is a good idea to include spouses and the church staff in the fellowship events.

Deacon Relationships With the Congregation

The relationships between deacons and the congregation they serve have two important dimensions. The first is a general relationship of the servant-leader to the people served. This is a positional relationship. The congregation recognizes the deacon as a spiritual model of the Christian lifestyle. Sometimes this relationship is limited to moderate exposure within the activities of the church body. In some cases, the only exposure occurs during the observance of the Lord's Supper.

The second dimension of the relationship develops as the deacon becomes involved in meeting the specific needs of the individual or family. Here, success requires a certain level of trust toward the deacon as minister. When the individual has almost no background with the deacon, barriers appear that significantly limits the effectiveness of the ministry effort.

Deacons create barriers to effective deacon ministries when they have limited contact with the congregation. To overcome these barriers, deacons must begin the relationship developmental process with the members the pastor assigns them to serve. The stronger the relationship, the greater the opportunity to provide an appropriate ministry during the time of need. We best facilitate this process by using an organized system of deacon assignments. The *Deacon Family Ministry Plan* is the most effective system available today. The local church decides the method it believes works best in building relationships and ministry.

The key to effective ministries is in the formation of as many bonds between the deacon and the church members as possible. The likelihood of a church member calling on the deacon, is proportionate to the strength of their relationship. Do not expect a family to allow a deacon to "come beside" them without an established relationship.

Deacons can nurture these relationships by visiting, or calling a person. Without prior contact, members will usually call their pastor, staff member, or the church office in general, rather than seeking help from a specific deacon.

Deacons and pastors work together in the ministry to the church. When a member calls a staff member for assistance, that staff member should include the deacon in the provision of help. If a need exists for a personal visit, the staff member, when possible, should include the deacon in the visit. If including the deacon in the initial visit is not possible, the staff member should contact the deacon for additional ministries and follow up. The more the church exposes the deacon to the needs of the family, the more likely they will feel comfortable calling the deacon directly in the future. This team-building effort allows for the expansion of ministry efforts.

The ultimate goal of the church is to involve every

member in a ministry. The deacon is the model of a personal ministry. The church will mobilize into an active ministry without seeing and hearing about the ministry efforts of the deacons. Likewise, as the deacons effectively serve, they stimulate the involvement of the total body in the ministry.

Deacon Relationships With the Community

Each deacon has the responsibility to display the qualities of the Christian Life before neighbors, friends, business associates, and all others in the community. The community itself can detect the serving spirit in the life of the deacon. Deacons are ready to serve individuals and families within the community at large as they identify needs.

When deacons build relationships with nonbelievers, they set an example for others in the church. If deacons only relate to fellow church members, the opportunity for personal evangelism is severely limited. If we expect the congregation to lead others to Christ, the deacon should be the model.

Deacon relationships form the basis for all ministry efforts. A failure here will result in ministry failures. Deacons grow in service and spirituality as they work within the structures of relationships.

5

♥ **A Sharpened Axe:**
The Expertise To "Come Beside"

Deacons gain the expertise to "come beside" through effective training and caring supervision. In some ministry fields, it is easier to find training events for secretaries and janitors than it is to find training for deacons. Likewise, many deacons do not have a mentor or person to supervise them. If churches will reverse these situations, they will gain deacons with the knowledge of how to "come beside" others in the ministry.

Effective Training Gives Deacons Expertise to Minister.

Involving the whole church in an annual study on the work of the deacons will clarify the congregation's expectations. Can we expect churches to elect or approve deacons without being fully exposed to the ministry expectations? The leaders who nominate deacons must understand the church's qualifications and selection process. Training the total church body in deacon ministries adds an important link that builds an effective ministry. The ideal time for this training would be just before a deacon election.

Regular training retreats or seminars will deepen the deacon's grasp of ministry skills required for the position. Without continuous effective training, the deacon ministry team has little hope to keep up with the demands of the task before them.

An informal survey, conducted in California in 1983, showed that more than 80% of the churches do not plan to provide regular deacon training. The same survey reported a 60% failure rate in *The Deacon Family Ministry Plan*. All of the churches reporting the failure of this ministry also reported that they provide no program of training for the deacons who are responsible for this significant ministry. A mere coincidence? Hardly. Churches that report these problems are similar to the list of churches that have no training.

Making changes in the ministry of deacons cannot succeed without a strong effort to establish ongoing deacon training programs. This explains why a deacon body can have strong, spiritually qualified and committed individuals, who fail in the performance of their duties. Though selecting qualified individuals is important, it is not enough, the deacons must have adequate training. The three most common reasons for failures in deacon ministries are: improper understanding of the Deaconship; overloading the work expectations, and lack of training.

Most churches offer "on the job training," but fail to give formal instruction. While this may be effective, it fails to meet the training needs of the newly elected deacon. On-the-job training is effective if the trainer has the right answers for all of the questions that might arise during the training period. Also, he must be a good example of an effective deacon, and can pass along the same level of effectiveness.

Other churches "give a book" to the deacon. But, there is a difference between having a book and reading it. How many unread books are on your shelf? Reading a book, though valuable to deacon training, does not insure that they actually absorb a clear understanding of the materials. Books alone are not enough.

Many suggest that each deacons' meeting should include at least fifteen minutes for deacon training updates. While this is healthy for updates, it in no way can provide the basic training deacons need in beginning the assigned ministry.

There are several resources available to provide the necessary materials for ongoing training efforts. Unfortunately, most churches fail to take advantage of these resources.

An additional problem occurs when a small portion of the deacon body receives instruction while others do not. One value of deacon training is keeping the total body of deacons, and the pastor, informed on the latest techniques to discover ministry needs of their people. A second value of deacon training, during the process of study, occurs as the pastor and deacons build stronger relationships.

I was leading a deacon training in Southern California, near where my parents lived, when I had the opportunity to train six deacons from First Southern Baptist Church of Downey, my parents' church. I taught them the team concept of Deacon ministry, including the need for a deacon to accompany the pastor on bereavement visits. If a deacon is along, he can call family members to notify them of the death of their loved one, while the pastor comforts the spouse. Little did I know at the time how much this training was about to impact me.

A few weeks later, I got a call at three o'clock in the morning. "Tom, Coy Byram here," I intuitively knew why he was calling; he was the chairman of the deacons at my parents' church. "I am very sorry to be the one that has to tell you this, but the Pastor is busy comforting your mother-- your father has just passed away." A few days later several deacons from his church were at the funeral.

Back home in Northern California, the deacons immediately began to minister to my family. The deacons "passed the hat" around and got enough money together to send one of the deacon's families to Southern California to attend the funeral. The cumulative ministry of these two deacon bodies made a very difficult time a little easier. Why do I believe in the importance of training? Because I've personally received the benefit of effective deacon ministries.

Deacon Training Today

Recognizing the failures of the past and the hope for the future should motivate each church to undertake the task of providing ongoing deacon training.[9] Effective instruction should include elements from a variety of sources and methods. Three essential areas in the training process are: the work of the church, the tasks of the deacon, and the personal dimension of the deacon. Keeping these three areas in balance will provide the opportunity for growth of the church, the ministry, and the personal development of the deacon.

---

[9]F. A. Agar, The deacon At Work, (Philadelphia: Judson Press, 1923) "Every local church should require the Deacons or deaconesses to attend a course of training conducted each year by the pastor." p. 23.

The deacon body can adopt a training schedule to insure that they include the variety of types and resources. The training schedule developed should cover the needs of the deacons for a three to a five-year time span. You must be careful to avoid an overemphasis on one of the three types of training while neglecting others.

Sample Training Schedule
YEAR ONE:

1. Schedule three Sunday evenings for the pastor to lead a series on deacon ministries for the total church body. You can devote Week One to the *vision* of the church, emphasizing the church's vision statement. The second week, the pastor can preach on the pastor--deacon team, showing how the deacons help the pastor and the total church in fulfilling its *vision*. During week three, the pastor can preach on the qualifications of the deacon, including the Biblical and church standards for the deacon.

To enhance the preaching, the pastor can use experienced deacons for testimonies or other teaching ideas. Good resources for weeks two and three could include selected chapters from Deacons: Servant Models in the Church and The Ministry of Baptist Deacons.

2. Schedule a weekend training event in January or February. This might be with sister churches. The materials might include one of the two books mentioned in the October Church-Wide Study. Tap into denominational resources for prospective leaders of the training.

3. Schedule a spring retreat to build relationships between

fellow deacons, pastor, or other staff persons. The resource materials might come from a specific book, such as Equipping Deacons as Partners in Ministry. The purpose of this retreat is to build new relationships between co-laborers, and to strengthen those already in existence.

4. Schedule a one day course on sharing the gospel of Jesus Christ. Involve leaders from the Sunday School or Evangelism Departments of the church. This one-day event will emphasize the importance of all Christians sharing their faith with the lost.

YEAR TWO:

1. Schedule a one-day study on a selected book related to the work of the church. The deacons could suggest the specific book and leader themselves. The purpose is to understand the work of the church and the participation of church leaders in that work.

2. Schedule a one-day study on the history of deacon ministry, or the relationship of the church to your denomination.

3. Schedule a weekend retreat with pastor and staff. Study conflict management and building relationships as it relates to the issue of conflict resolution.

4. Schedule a one day study on the specific work of the deacons in your own church. This could include such topics as: The Deacons and The Lord's Supper, The Deacons and Baptism, and a review of the plan adopted by the deacons and the church for ministry to the total body.

YEAR THREE:

Conduct a retreat where the deacon body analyzes their

needs and develops a calender of training for the year.

Other Training Suggestions

In some areas, intensive training schedules are appropriate. Intensive training might include six three-hour sessions spread over a twelve-week period. A deacon training specialist has often conducted a session using this method sponsored by their denomination.

On-the-job training can be very helpful to new deacons in conjunction with the other training opportunities. Ideally, assign the new deacon to observe three or four different deacons throughout their first year of service. This exposes the new deacon to more than one model for service.

Each deacons' meeting could also include a short training update or review. This not only helps each deacon to improve their individual skills, but may open the door to new avenues of ministry.

Every deacon training event should include the spouse of all involved. Often the church best facilitates the work of the deacon through the joint effort of husband and wife teams.

The most important concern is that the church consistently makes training available to every deacon. The deacon chairman can negotiate specific scheduling of dates for each event with the deacon body to be sure that every deacon possible is present. The chairman can announce upcoming events.

Supervision Gives Deacons Expertise to Minister.

Why do churches not discuss the issue of deacon

supervision? Early in adulthood, most people learn to fear supervision. Has your heart ever pounded through your chest when you heard, "The supervisor wants to see you?" In reality, the supervisor that cautions, scolds, or even fires the employee is the same person who offers praise and pay increases for those who do well. Supervisors are the people who help us advance in our careers. So, why do we fear them?

What is the purpose of supervision? Dr. Doran McCarty introduced a definition of supervision that is commonly accepted in the field of seminary education and in mission fields at home and abroad. "Supervision is, the development of a support system for the enrichment of personhood and to assist in the performance of tasks.[10]"

McCarty sees supervision as a positive interaction. His approach is purely positive even though most people think of the word in a negative light. This positive understanding of supervision is applicable to deacon ministries.

As we seek to introduce intentional supervision into the deacon program, we must understand that the church supervises the deacon from several directions. The most logical supervisor is the chairman of the deacons. The church provides further supervision through the input of pastor and staff. The church body that selects deacons also reserves authority to oversee their work.

10Doran C. McCarty, Supervising Ministry Students (Atlanta: Home Mission Board, SBC, 1978) p. 9.

Values of Good Supervision

Good supervision is valuable in building the personal lives of those involved. The supervision system supports those whose lives become more willing to do the assigned tasks. Here are five direct values of good supervision:

1. It says that the job is important.

We rarely supervise jobs that are unimportant. When workers complete an assigned task, they expect some form of acknowledgment. Deacons should feel that their job is important. Those in the supervisory roles provide the recognition of the service to the congregation provided by the effective deacon.

2. It says that the person is important.

Every deacon has the need to hear from the supervisor when a task is 'well done.' Likewise, they need to hear from the supervisor when a correction is necessary in the performance of the tasks. Reminders of our need for improvement in areas of ministry say that the supervisor wants us to become the best we can be in the ministry.

3. It produces intentional ministries.

Supervision provides opportunities for the exercising of individual gifts in providing service to the people. The deacon is most effective when seeking people that need help, and then taking the actions to meet those needs.

4. It provides a continuous system of support.

Deacons should never have the feeling that they are alone in the work of the ministry. Supervision encourages the workers. Those in supervision are resource persons when the deacon is unsure of the appropriate actions to take. Deacons are not exempt from the need to receive ministry from others. Good supervisors discover needs in the lives of deacons, and initiates necessary care.

5. It establishes the criteria for accountability and evaluation.

We all work effectively when we are held accountable for our efforts. One purpose of monthly meetings is to receive reports of ministry activities. This form of accountability is not only visible to the supervisor, but further helps the deacon to do self evaluations.

Values of Good Supervisory Meetings

On occasion, the supervisor should meet privately with each deacon. The supervisor uses this opportunity to provide a time of evaluation of the performance of duties and gives the deacons an equal opportunity to express any concerns that they may have.

Good supervisory meetings provide a method of resolving problems created through misunderstandings. The following values are the result of the regularly scheduled supervisory sessions:

1. It serves to clarify expectations of the ministry.
2. It provides opportunities for reinforcement of the objectives of Deacon ministry.
3. It reduces stressful confrontations.
4. It provides a healthy forum for course corrections or recognition of accomplishments.

Deacon ministry in every church should include a process for supervision of groups and individuals. The supervisor replaces the fear of supervision, by showing the contribution it makes to the overall effectiveness of the program. Good supervision and effective training will give deacons the expertise they need to "come beside."

6

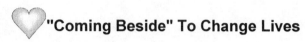"Coming Beside" To Change Lives

The greatest rewards of deacon ministries come when they "come beside" others in need. They "come beside" people with what they say, what they do, and who they are.

Deacons proclaim the Gospel

Jesus told us to pray to the Lord of the harvest that he would "thrust" laborers into the field. I was a new pastor in my first church when a deacon did more than pray--he "thrust" me into the harvest himself.

We were visiting with the man of the house in the living room, while his wife clattered around in the kitchen. We talked about the weather, sports, current events and everything else I could think of. That is, we talked about everything, except the gospel. Finally, my visitation partner, a deacon trainee, interrupted the conversation. I saw a bit of fire in his eyes when he asked, "pastor, didn't we come here to tell this man about Christ?" "Well--yes," I stammered. "Then when are you going to get around to it?"

I did the best I could to present the gospel that evening. Finally, I asked the man if he wished to follow Christ. He declined. From the kitchen, I heard his wife's timid reply, "I would." His response surprised me. He listened so intently, I fully expected him to accept Christ. His wife's response startled me. I didn't even know she was listening.

I quickly reviewed the Gospel message with her and led her in the sinner's prayer. I will never forget that evening.

Over the years, I've tried to return the favor and "thrust" deacons into the harvest. Usually, I begin by taking them with me to observe my witness; then, when the time is right, I encourage them to present the Gospel.

Gary and I were visitation partners for several months. He watched me lead several people to Christ and always rejoiced when someone prayed the "sinner's prayer." The first time we led someone to the Lord, he drove the car around the corner from their home, put the car in park and walked in front of it. He jumped in the air, clicking his heels together and exclaimed "YES!" He was hooked.

Gary and his wife were cultivating some friends, hoping to see them come to Christ. He invited them over to his home for lunch one Saturday afternoon with the intention of directing the conversation toward spiritual matters. He told me that I should casually "drop by" about 2:00 because he would have them ready for me to present the plan of Salvation and pray the sinner's prayer with them.

"Gary," I said, "that sounds like a fine plan. I'm so glad you've worked with this family and are concerned about their souls, but there's a problem." "What's the problem?" Gary asked. "Well, there's a football game Saturday afternoon and I'll not be coming by your house." "You mean you'd miss an opportunity to lead someone to Christ over a football game?"

"You've watched me lead numerous people to Christ over the past few months, haven't you?" "Well . . . yes." "You know the plan of Salvation as well as I do, don't you?" "Well . . . yes." "Then you share the gospel and you pray the sinner's prayer with them. I'll be by the phone if you need me."

I did get a call that afternoon, but not at 2:00. At 4:00, Gary called me to report that not only did the husband and wife accept Christ that day, but the two teenage children did too. The entire family of four was reborn in Gary's living room. I wonder how high Gary jumped when they left the house?

A few years later, Gary's eighteen year old son was my visitation partner after a witnessing seminar for new teachers. On the way to our visit, I asked him if he felt confident enough to share the plan of salvation. He said he was ready and I told him I'd be his prayer partner. He did a fine job. First, he shared the difference Christ made in his life, then he explained how to accept Christ. He did not, however, ask the person to pray the sinner's prayer. I stepped in and prayed with the young man.

We got in the car to drive away. My visitation partner drove around the block, put the car in park, and walked to the front of the car. You guessed it--he jumped in the air, clicking his heels together and exclaimed "YES!" He was hooked--just like his father; he was hooked. Before his 30th birthday, he followed in his father's footsteps and became a deacon.

Proclamation of the Gospel is not the exclusive domain of the pastor. Deacons "come beside" the pastor to lead the entire congregation to share the gospel with the community.

The eighth chapter of Acts describes a major turning point in the history of the early church, with the genesis of the persecution of the early church. "And Saul was consenting unto his death. And at that time there was a great persecution against the church which was at Jerusalem. They were all scattered abroad throughout the regions of Judaea and Samaria, except the apostles."[11]

Some Christians would rather pay a professional than to become involved in personal evangelism. In effect, this is the ministry by proxy. [12] Most people feel more confident leaving such an important task to the professionals.[13] However, a ministry cannot be done effectively by proxy. "A layperson cannot pay someone else to fulfill his or her ministry for God.

11

Acts 8:1, KJV

12

D. James Kennedy, Evangelism Explosion (Wheaton, Illinois: Tyndale House Publishers, 1970), "So successful has Satan been with this strategy that it has been estimated that probably 95 percent of American church members have never led anyone to Christ. Thus the army of Christ has been more than decimated and the response from the pew has been, 'Let Clerical George do it.'" p. 4.

13

Frank R. Tillapaugh, Unleashing the Church (Ventura: Regal Books, 1982), p. 92.

God has called His people to the ministry, and the ministry belongs to the laity whether they know it or not."[14]

What was the Spirit's strategy? Everyone except the professionals, the apostles, went out to spread the gospel. As persecution dispersed the church, people could propagate the gospel everywhere they went. The Christians went out and did the evangelizing. Owen Cooper calls this an equivalent to a modern "simultaneous evangelistic crusade."[15]

Who remained to evangelize Jerusalem? Who could talk to the scribes, Sadducees, Pharisees and others with a high degree of education? The best-trained men were left behind to deal with Jerusalem and to sustain a training post for other Christians.

Deacons who "come beside" their pastor, do not reduce the pastor's role in the church, they restore him to his Biblical position as a trainer [16] of the Saints and to the dignity God

---

[14]

Findley B. Edge, The Doctrine of the Laity (Nashville: Convention Press, 1985), p. 46.

[15]

Fisher Humphreys, Thomas A. Kinchen, eds. Laos: All the People of God, (New Orleans: New Orleans Baptist Theological Seminary, 1984), The Need, by Owen Cooper, p. 9.

[16]

Ephesians 4:11-12, NASB "And He gave some as apostles,

intended for the office.[17]

There are times when a pastor cannot preach and needs a deacon to "come beside" him to proclaim the gospel in public. What would happen in your church next Sunday if your pastor became suddenly ill? Who would preach? Perhaps you have other staff members or a retired pastor in your congregation. If you do, your pastor probably has a plan in place to cover such an event. If you don't, then your pastor might ask you to preach. Are you ready?

Pastor Miller was sick. He successfully preached the morning services and attended the committee meetings scheduled for Sunday afternoon, but he just couldn't muster up the strength the handle the evening service. His throat was closing down; it felt like someone was choking him. His voice was scratchy, and he could not project beyond a hoarse whisper. After the last meeting of the afternoon, he grabbed one of his deacons by the arm and said, "I can't preach tonight. Can you handle it?" With just a few hours warning,

---

and some as prophets, and some as evangelists, and some as pastors and teachers, for the equipping of the saints for the work of service, to the building up of the Body of Christ."

[17]

R. Paul Stevens, <u>Liberating the Laity</u> (Downers Grove, Illinois: InterVarsity Press, 1985), "This does not mean the demotion of the pastor and the promotion of the so-called layperson. For through equipping, both pastor and layperson are restored to their proper dignity." p. 10.

the deacon "came beside" his pastor and preached the evening sermon.[18]

The role of the lay preacher is an important part of Baptist history. They have not required educational nor denominational credentials to perform pastoral functions. In 1746 a query came to the Philadelphia Association asking: "Query from the Church of Philadelphia: Whether it be lawful or regular for any person to preach the gospel publicly without ordination? Answer: that which we have both rule and precedent for in the word of God, is, and must be, both lawful and regular."[19]

Deacons Serve the People

Deacons "come beside" their pastor to administer the ordinances of the church to the people. No moment of church life shows the teamwork of the pastor and deacons or shows the servant heart of church leaders more than the observance of the Lord's Supper. As Jesus took the bread and the cup and gave it to His Apostles, modern church leaders follow His example and serve their congregation in memory of Him.

---

[18]

Duane Miller, Out of the Silence (Nashville: Thomas Nelson Publishers, 1996)

[19]

A.D. Gillette, ed., Minutes of the Philadelphia Baptist Association (Minneapolis: A.M. James Publishing Co., 1851), p. 50-51.

Some congregations extend the service of the Lord's Supper to its shut-ins who cannot attend the regular worship services of the church. The deacons meet at the church on Sunday afternoon and go to the homes of the shut-ins and administer the Lord's Supper to them. They share greetings from the shut-ins with the congregation during the evening service.

Service does not end with administering the ordinances of the church. Let's face it; not every deacon will feel comfortable preaching, teaching or witnessing. Some would rather serve with their hands.

A deacon in Central California runs an automobile ministry for his church. He does routine repairs for widows and single women who need assistance. He does safety checks on their cars and advises them when they should take their car to a garage for a major repair. On two different occasions, he got old "junker" cars running and gave them to impoverished families who needed basic transportation.

Another deacon in West Texas would discover needs while visiting with the shut-ins. Perhaps it was a leaky roof, or a dripping faucet or a sprung screen door. Whatever the need, he would show up with other men from the church to repair the problem. He didn't talk about serving the congregation. He did it!

Serving the Lord's Supper is the most visible ministry of the deacon. It shows his servant's heart. Other not so visible ministries take place daily as deacons "come beside" those in need.

Deacons Set an Example

Deacon ministries do not end with what a deacon says or does, it includes who he is. Though both proclamation and service are important, neither can define a deacon's ministry. Deacons are examples. A deacon is someone a new husband can observe to see how to treat his bride. Deacons are models of spirituality and dedication to their church. Perhaps their greatest ministry is the high standards they set for themselves and the way they live their lives before others.

Deacons are role models for other lay ministers in the church. By definition, the deacons are a "Lay Ministry Team." The differences between the deacon body and other ministry teams are the standards they must meet for eligibility to minister. Though specific churches differ in their standards, most would agree that:

- Deacons are exclusively male
- Most churches exclude divorced persons, either completely or they are subjected to careful study of the circumstances leading to their divorced status.
- Single persons are often not considered.
- Those who are new in the faith cannot serve.

Other lay ministers do not have to meet these guidelines, nor do they hold the same "status" deacons hold in the church. When deacons live an exemplary Christian life, they help raise the standards of other lay ministers.

Deacons are catalysts that help change peoples' lives when they minister to them. God uses what they say when they proclaim the gospel, what they do when they serve, and how they live to make a difference in the life of their church, pastor, community and world.

7

♡ "Coming Beside"
To Keep Your Church Healthy

They said Jesus is a drunk, and Paul is not really an apostle and that anyone can do Moses' job. Your church is in good company if it has conflict.

Conflict will always exist in the church, because sinful people attend church. The deacon body must manage the conflict before it overtakes the ministry of the church. Every deacon holds two buckets--one bucket of gas, and another with water. When a conflict flares, he can either add fuel to the fire by throwing gas on it, or put water on it and put out the fire. The church depends on the deacon body to minimize the damage of the conflict. How does a deacon put water on the fire?

Deacons Don't Protect the Anonymous Source

Journalists must protect the sources for their stories or they will dry up. Some journalist will even go to jail instead of revealing their sources. Deacons, however, do not protect their sources. A friend came to Pastor Bruce's office to verify or dismiss a troubling rumor that questioned his character. She told him the rumor and the name of the person spreading it. Immediately, he reached for the phone.

"Hi, this is Pastor Bruce, I have Nancy in my office and she tells me that you are saying . . ." Can you imagine the reaction? He got a fast apology. The only reason Pastor Bruce could solve this problem was that Nancy told him the source of the rumor.

Why do people wish to remain anonymous, yet feel free to spread rumors or stir up conflict? They want **you** to fight, while they sit back and watch the fireworks. The scripture warns against such people in Proverbs 6:16-19

[16] These six things doth the Lord hate: yea, seven are an abomination unto him: [17] A proud look, a lying tongue, and hands that shed innocent blood, [18] An heart that deviseth wicked imaginations, feet that be swift in running to mischief, [19] A false witness that speaketh lies, and he that soweth discord among brethren.

They actually have more power to stir conflict if they remain anonymous. "Pastor, some people are saying . . ." sounds more ominous than, "Pastor, Sister Jones, who voted against your call because she wanted her nephew to be our pastor is saying . . . " Truth can stand the scrutiny of the light of day. Secrecy keeps the conflict going and the parties from resolving their differences.

The scripture teaches that disputing parties should meet in private to resolve their differences before involving other people in Matthew 18:15-17.

Moreover if thy brother shall trespass against thee, go and tell him his fault between thee and him alone: if he shall hear thee, thou hast gained thy brother. [16] But if he will not hear thee, then take with thee one or two more, that in the mouth of two or three witnesses every word may be established. [17] And if he shall neglect to hear them, tell it unto the church: but if he neglect to hear the church, let him be unto thee as an heathen man and a publican.

If the deacon carries a complaint without revealing the source, he is violating the clear instruction of the scripture.

If the charge is against the pastor or other leader, the scripture teaches that it cannot be considered without two witnesses. "But if he will not hear thee, then take with thee one or two more, that in the mouth of two or three witnesses every word may be established" (Matthew 18:16) A witness is not an anonymous whisperer, rather, it is a person with a name and a face. How can a church confront a legitimate problem if people will not come forward in the open? They can't. If someone comes to you with a problem, yet wishes to remain anonymous, tell them that you cannot hear their complaint unless they allow you to approach the parties involved with all the facts, including their name. You also need to tell them that you will probably instigate a meeting for them to work out their differences.

Deacons Keep the Conflict Private

When conflict comes, it is tempting to publicly correct the misinformation; it doesn't work. The "bully pulpit," escalates the problem; it doesn't squash the rumor.

Pastor Martinez inherited some money from a church member. He felt it was God's grace in his life to provide for his retirement. Rumors spread.

He called a special meeting of the church to "clear the air." It didn't work; people's minds were fixed on their position.

They said mean, hurtful things. The pastor resigned shortly thereafter.

"Going public" with the problem spreads the seeds of discord where they did not previously exist, and gives it more credibility than it deserves. Using the grapevine is far better than the microphone. This pastor's ministry did not have to end. The deacons could have helped if they made home visits to those who thought there was impropriety.

Our custom was to cancel the Easter Sunday night service. One year, during our business meeting, we had a particularly lively discussion about the issue. A deacon, who recently transferred into our church, adamantly opposed closing the service and spoke against it. He thought it would damage our witness for Christ in the community. Because of his concern, we voted to have the evening service.

A few weeks later, Easter rolled around and we had a huge attendance on Sunday morning; it was standing room only. It was a glorious morning, but that evening, we only had eight present. Five of the eight were members of my family. Among those absent was the deacon who had made it such an issue.

At the next deacons meeting, I brought the item up and suggested if the deacons had strong feelings on an issue and made it so known, they better be willing to support it. I said, "Don't vote for things unless you are willing to support it with your attendance." Everyone knew who I was talking about.

The man got so angry that he eventually pulled his family out of the church and went elsewhere. Though we tried to intervene with home visits, we lost the family for good. I still believe he was wrong, but maybe I could have salvaged this family by confronting him in private instead of in a public meeting.

"Church problems" are not the topic of small talk or casual conversation. Deacons must use caution when discussing them with other people. Share the problems on a "need to know" basis only. Confidentiality is an important element of conflict management. Without it, the deacon will escalate the conflict and hurt the people involved.

Deacons Confront Conflict

Helen was a new member of the church who seemed a bit pushy. Within a month of joining the church, she came into the pastor's office with a list of demands for changes in the nursery. Her suggestions seemed reasonable, and Pastor Brent was appreciative that she brought the deficiencies to his attention. We made the changes and he thought that was the end of the matter. What the pastor did not know at the time is that she boasted to the nursery workers about how fast she could get things done. They resented the implication that she could do what they could not do for themselves. Her gloating caused major discontentment among the nursery employees. Because of the conflict, one resigned.

The next week, the secretary walked into the pastor's office on a "do not disturb day." She said, "I just got off the phone with Helen. She is very upset about a decision the Church Council made last night, she says we don't care about missions because we are not promoting the Easter Offering. She wants to talk to you." A flash of anger seized Brent, who thought "who does she think she is? She has no right to question the council!" He was beginning to understand that she wanted the church to fit the mold of her church back East.

When the pastor returned Helen's call concerning the Council meeting, he could not hear a word she was saying. He immediately became defensive and outraged at her suggestion that the Church Council is not sensitive to missions. Brent perceived that she would be at his office door with a new challenge each week. The phone call did not end well; Helen slammed the phone on the receiver while Brent was still talking.

The conflict with Helen escalated in the coming months. She was vocal about her discontent with the pastor and the church. She launched a "phone campaign," complaining to whomever would listen. Helen whispered in the halls, and yelled in business meetings. She attacked every authority figure she could, and she drew blood.

She consumed the pastor's schedule. If he wasn't listening to her complain about the church, he was listening to the church leaders complain about her. Brent met with her husband on a couple of occasions to see if they could resolve the problems. He decided they all needed to sit together, so they scheduled a meeting.

The meeting was emotional. They confronted the issues and wept, but resolved nothing; things already had gone too far. The husband said, "Pastor, it appears that Helen is as much at fault in this matter as anyone, and we are sorry for that. If we could only have solved this before it went this far we could remain in the church, but now, we must leave."

Then he asked, "Why didn't we get a visit from the deacons when this problem was brewing? Isn't that what deacons are for?"

The answer to that question is yes! Because the pastor was involved in the conflict, he was not an objective spiritual leader. The deacons needed to step in to bring some control and order to the problem. At the end, Helen learned what she did wrong and changed her behavior at her next church. It is too bad she didn't learn before she burned her bridges and had to move her membership.

Pastors and deacons should be mutually supportive, especially at times when they are under attack by someone in the congregation. In one church I served, we adopted a policy requiring that neither the deacon nor pastor would agree with any criticisms received against the other. The person receiving a complaint would acknowledge the complaint, but would encourage the person to make any complaint directly to the person involved. If this were not acceptable, it was up to the person to contact the pastor or deacon and discuss the matter openly. Our commitment to each other was that if the complaint was justified, we would undertake immediate action to rectify the situation. The party receiving the complaint was kept informed until all were satisfied, and we resolved the issue. Problems not addressed promptly will most likely grow larger as time progresses.

Sources of Conflict

The issue at the heart of the conflict is usually an honest difference of opinion. Perhaps it relates to church finances or other issues that appear during times of change in the make-up, activities, or leadership structure of the church.

Personality differences often overshadow the importance of the issue at the center of conflict. People usually side with friends despite the issue under consideration and naturally fall on the opposing sides with people they've fought with before.

People don't always fight over big issues. In one business meeting, I watched the church approve its largest budget ever, almost without question, unanimously. Five minutes later in the same session, a dispute occurred over the purchase of a six-dollar volleyball. The debate lasted more than thirty minutes, but the conflict never really ended.

Results of Conflict

Conflict can ultimately result in the closing of a church, or to a healthy resolution where God's grace reconciles all parties and strengthens relationships. Between the extremes are a variety of symptoms, each with its own level of emotional stress. Every conflict results in anger, pain, withdrawal, aggressive behavior, loss of control, divisions, and strife.

Unresolved conflict brings the spirit of the church down. A sister church a few miles away from mine seemed always to have a conflict going. Finally, with only ten or twelve members left, they voted to disband the church and close its doors for the final time. Immediately, some of their members began to visit our church. I made a home visit on one of the leadership families that visited our church. The wife described their visit in our worship as, ". . . the first time in sixteen years that they felt the presence of God during a worship service; our worship services always contained a feeling of tension and the exchange of glares among the members."

Before conflict inflicts this kind of pain in the church, deacons need to confront the problem and introduce God's grace into the bickering. The book, Equipping Deacons To Confront Conflict, is a great source of finding the Biblical patterns to employ to resolve conflict. Widespread conflict in the church may create the need to seek help from an outside source. Your denomination can help you find or provide the necessary help.

Deacons need to take every expression of conflict in the church seriously. The longer the conflict remains before resolution, the greater opportunity for its rapid growth. Though most people do not enjoy confrontation, it is an absolute necessity to bring peace in the midst of a storm. Allowing conflict to remain without resolution can undo the positive contributions achieved by the church and block its future opportunities. Confrontation, accompanied by a spirit of love, with the desire for reconciliation of all parties will protect your church from the effects of prolonged conflict.

8

"Coming Beside"
Will Communicate The Ministry Of Your Church

Organizations within the church often wonder why more people are not involved in their groups. The Women's missionary circle questions why the young women do not attend their meetings. Choir directors want more people in the choir lofts.

The problem of poor participation is a result of poor communication. The church office replies, "It is in the weekly bulletin, our published newsletter, and we announce the meetings from the pulpit. What more can we do?" We can do a lot more is the real answer. The church achieves the best communication through personal sharing. No group in the church is better prepared to facilitate the solution than the deacons.

Some years ago two new couples joined our church through a profession of faith and baptism. All four had little or no previous church experience. Shortly after joining the church, they attended a "night out" fellowship at a local restaurant hosted by an adult Sunday School class. They sat together at the end of the long table prepared for the group of around thirty participants. My wife and I selected the seats closest to theirs. The couple decided to share a bottle of wine with the Italian meal they ordered. This was the first church event I had ever attended where someone drank wine. No one said anything to the couple, though everyone noticed. On the way home, my wife and I discussed the issue and quickly agreed that the couple had done nothing wrong.

The next day a longtime member of the church came to the office early . . . and stayed late. She challenged everything about the event, from the ordering of the wine to my lack of response, and even to my call to ministry and Christian experience. How dare I allow this to happen in her church! Later, one of the four new members reported that they had all noticed mixed reactions to the wine bottle in front of them at the table. His concern was whether or not we would allow them to return to the church. Both responses to the event provided no small dispute in my own reflections on the evening.

I do not think this couple was in the wrong. If anyone was wrong, it was the leadership of the church. No one told this new couple that Baptist people do not usually drink alcohol in front of one another. Though it is common for an anti drinking sermon or Sunday School lesson, we had not had one since they joined the church. Besides, can the church expect more from new members than we taught them?

I felt that if any apologies are in order, the responsibility rests with the church to apologize for any actions of the membership that put the new members in an uncomfortable position. The problems and misunderstandings were soon corrected to the satisfaction of all. There is no guarantee, however, that assures us that resolving all future issues will be easy.

What have we learned from the issues and questions presented? One lesson is evident. The church has a definite responsibility to communicate all of its doctrines, policies, programs and goals with new and old members.

Deacons communicate with the Members

No one person or group in the church should be more familiar with the overall teachings and programs of the church than the deacons. Their faithful participation in church life and their role as leaders requires that they know and understand the work of the church. They will not attend all of the activities of the church, but they should be able to tell others how the church can include them in the activity.

Establishing contact with new and old members provides the opportunity for deacons to communicate upcoming church events. Personal sharing about church events, and teachings is the best source of information to the total body. Since the work of the deacons focuses on personal contact with every member, being the front line of communication is reasonable for them.

Recognizing that communication is both "hearing and telling," deacons should be as effective in listening as they are at speaking. Listening is more than a pause from speaking. It is a chance to understand the message the speaker is conveying.

Empathetic listening is important. Empathy is not sympathy. Sympathetic listening involves feeling the emotions and understanding the logic of the speaker. Empathetic listening feels the pain and gets involved in finding a solution to the problem of the speaker. It is active, not passive.

As the church receives new members into the body, the pastor assigns a deacon to make a home visit. During this visit, a deacon can learn much about the experiences of the new member and how they see themselves fitting into their new church. These times of discovery provide the opportunity for the new member to become active participants in the work of the church, rather than waiting for a future opportunity.

Deacons do not necessarily have all the answers, but they can refer the member to the person with the information. A person who joins the church by transfer from a sister church in another city may bring with them years of experience in teaching children. They may be eager to continue that service in the new community. By bringing the Sunday School Director into contact with this new member immediately, both receive a benefit. The director may get a new or future teacher and the new members may get an opportunity to fulfill their calling as a teacher.

Deacons can make friends in every area of church life when they refer potential workers, teachers, or music participants to the leaders of various church ministries.

The assimilation of new members into total church life is the result of their early participation in various activities. Deacons strive to discover the needs of the new member in areas of growth or service and then make appropriate referrals to meet those needs. The communication of prayer concerns and specific ministry opportunities to all members will serve to maximize the participation in prayer and ministry.

Deacons Communicate With the Pastor

Sometimes the deacons "come beside" the pastor to serve as a sounding board for ideas. They provide the feedback a pastor needs to evaluate ideas.

One Sunday morning, in the deacons' prayer time before the service, I shared that God was speaking to me about changing the Order of Worship. "I want to begin the service with the invitation instead of the Call to Worship. I just believe that I don't need to preach in order for the Spirit to work." To be honest, I anticipated a reaction of "you want to do what?"

Though some of the men did raise some concern about whether it was the right thing to do, there was no argument in the deacons' meeting. They agreed that if the Holy Spirit led, I would have to follow the Holy Spirit. We prayed and left the room.

Dick Lindsey stayed behind and stopped me while everyone else was leaving the room. He closed the door and put his arm around me and said "Pastor, I want to tell you something. If the Holy Spirit leads you to start with the invitation, then you better listen to the Holy Spirit and not to us. When I get up in the choir loft, I am going to pray that you will follow the Lord's leading."

I began the service with a time of announcements and then extended the invitation. I stepped down to the center aisle as the invitation started, but before the congregation could sing the first line, I heard a little commotion and looked up to see a young couple running down the aisle. I had never seen anything like it.

This young couple came from another Southern Baptist

Church about fifteen to twenty miles away. They moved into our community and were church shopping. They ran down the aisle with tears in their eyes and smiles on their faces. "What kind of decision did you come to make?" They said "We want to move our letter here right now."

The man said that earlier that morning, they went to a church about two miles North of us, pulled into the parking lot and realized they were about ten minutes early. He and his wife looked at each other and he said to her, "Why are we here?" She said, "We decided we were going to visit all the churches before we joined one." He said "Yeah, but isn't it better to follow the Lord and join the one God wants us to join rather than the one we think best?" She said "Well-- yes!" "I think it is obvious God wants us to join that church we went to before" (referring to our church). "I agree," she said, "I am with you! I think the Holy Spirit is directing us there for sure." "We have ten minutes, so let's go there and join the church today." They prayed in the parking lot of another church, started the car and came to ours. When the invitation started he took her by the hand and ran down the aisle (which wasn't a small feat for a woman who was seven months pregnant). They came with tears in their eyes and asked for membership in the church. He said to me, "Pastor, the Holy Spirit is really working today." I asked, "What do you mean?" He said "Well we made our decision in the parking lot north of town, and on the way here I drove in a hurry. I wanted to be sure we got here. To tell you the truth I don't know if we could have waited all the way through the service to make our decision. To have it at the beginning of the service is just what we wanted and needed."

As I sat them down, I looked up and saw that the aisle was completely full. Right behind this couple was a Black couple we were praying for. That morning they were on their way to the Black church across town from us but were running late. As they came across the bridge, they could see the top of our church from the bridge. They looked at each other and said, "You know we promised to visit the Black Church and we went a couple of times. We need to follow the leadership of the Lord. Yes, and we are running late today. Why don't we just go back to the Multiracial Church and see if maybe God doesn't want us there?" So when the invitation started, they immediately heard God's voice, and they responded.

When I finished with them, directly behind them was another couple. The woman had been a member of the church for about eight years by this time but the husband had never received Christ (In fact, he thought himself to be an atheist). That particular Sunday morning the Holy Spirit moved in his life, and he was bawling like a baby.

The invitation took one hour, there were nineteen decisions, nine for baptism and ten joined the church by letter or statement. At the end of the invitation, it was a little after twelve, I asked them if they wanted to dismiss in prayer and go home or should we start our regular service. It was unanimous, they wanted to stay and have the rest of the service as planned. After the message, I extended a second invitation. Another couple responded.

I am grateful for a deacon that "came beside" me that day to encourage me to follow the leadership of the Holy Spirit.

70

He gave me the affirmation I needed to do what I thought God was leading me to do.

9

"Coming Beside" To Influence Others

The Life Cycle of the Church

We can trace the importance of every church having a current Vision Statement through the "Life Cycle of the Church" model. This model explains how churches move from the inception, through the stages of life, to death. The following stages explain the elements and results that the church realizes during that period. The information a church gains about its own condition will help them find necessary corrections to return to their most healthy state.

Vision

During this stage, the church develops a carefully thought-out statement regarding the purpose that led to the establishment of the congregation. Sometimes churches call this a Vision Statement, Mission Statement, or Purpose Statement. This vision produces a high level of excitement as the members sense a closeness to the calling of God that will be completed through this body of believers. This excitement creates a willingness to make sacrifices in giving, time, and effort.

Organization

Vision, and the commitment it creates, leads to the formation of an organizational plan to direct the church as it strives toward fulfillment. During organization, the church establishes budgets, forms committees, and chooses programs. Time and prayer is directed toward the selection of persons who will lead the various elements of the organization.

Work

With the structure in place and the commitment level high, the members direct their energies toward the "work of the church," such as preaching, teaching, leading, prayer, fellowship, ministries, etc. Work and sacrifice combine to move the church toward its ultimate goals.

Mission

Mission, sometimes called the "mission accomplished" stage, occurs when the church is up and running. The church often realizes its original goals during this phase. Mission includes a time of celebration over the accomplishments. With the fulfillment of vision comes a reduction in excitement and the willingness to sacrifice. They presume it to no longer be a necessity. Too often this stage produces a feeling of indifference toward the work.

Maintenance

Maintenance follows closely behind completion. The body no longer makes future plans. Rather, they narrow their focus to keeping the past alive. When they chart their church attendance, it looks like the teeth of a saw; up for a period of time; down for the next. The nominating committee uses the same sheets to find the same number of classes, and to fill the same number of committee spaces. Finance committees look for ways to cut the budget or at best, to meet the same levels of giving as the year before. They replace all excitement with the need to maintain. Maintenance is neither hot nor cold; at best, it is lukewarm. The maintenance may be of short duration or in some cases, go on for years. No matter the time period, it leads to decline.

Decline

Decline means decline! Attendance, giving, programming, missions, etc., all stagger downward. The church tries to stop the decline spiral, but usually without success. The church refocuses its efforts. No longer looking to the future, it begins to seek places or people to blame for the decline. If serious candidates for blame cannot be found outside the church, they soon seek them within. The church may encourage their pastor to leave or dismiss him. They may replace or reorganize deacons. No leaders are exempt from the search for a scapegoat for the problems.

The church is no longer in harmony. Groups or divisions begin to appear. Two classes of members soon emerge: the re enforcers and the questioners. The re enforcers hold the traditional line believing that no changes are necessary. While at the same time, the questioners seek to discover the cause behind the decline. Questioners most often demand change. One of these two groups will prevail, resulting in the disappearance of the other group. If the questioners prevail, the re enforcers seek a church that operates in the traditional mold. Questioners will seek a more contemporary church that is open to new methods and styles.

Strong feelings of tension mark decline. Soon the church directs its energy toward the disharmony generated by the decline, rather than finding solutions to the problem.

Struggle to Survive

We mark the final stages of decline by the beginning of the struggle to survive. Like any living creature, some parts will fight to insure it breathes its final breath with dignity. Those who stay to the end must decide how the church will die. The remaining members will begin to dispose of church properties and equipment, while seeking to preserve the church's memory. Usually the local association becomes the benefactor of the remaining assets.

Death

Death is the final stage of the "Life Cycle." I have observed this dying process in other churches on several occasions. Interestingly, in some cases the observers say, "It is about time," or "I wondered how long it would survive." Others comment on "what they did wrong," or what they could have done to avoid death. People find little comfort in such comments.

The loss of a church is a serious matter. Many members completely fall away from the church. Others will never return to the same commitment level that they previously experienced.

The only alternative to death is to "re dream the dream." Each church should ask itself, "What is our mission?" The Mission Statement for any church establishes the purpose for its initial establishment and reasons for continuing as a church of The Lord Jesus Christ.

Some churches fail to recognize the true purpose of its ongoing existence. Other times, we establish churches with a Vision or Purpose Statement but fail to communicate that vision with the church as a whole. Often a church built upon a legitimate Vision Statement loses sight of that vision by increasing in membership without sharing the vision with any new members added to the original body. A church without a Vision or Purpose Statement soon becomes a body whose members function solely for perpetuating the organization.

Every church needs to rethink their Mission or Vision Statement regularly, making changes or adjustments as needed. The church must share their Vision or Mission Statement with the current membership and with every new member upon their acceptance into the body. Overlooking this important communication will create a stale church ministry.

Deacons have several responsibilities to help the church develop a relevant Vision Statement. They can help initiate the process, if it does not have one. The deacons also have input on the Vision Statement at times when it is under revision or in the adoption process. Secondly, deacons should know the Vision Statement to help in the interpretation of the statement for the benefit of both old and new church members. The Vision Statement is a vital part in the establishment of the total church program. The better we inform the congregation of the statement and its application, the more likely they are to participate in the fulfillment of its objectives.

Thirdly, deacons in their leadership role, are both participants in the process of working toward the goals of the church and encouragers of the total congregation in committing to and working on the common efforts of the church. If deacons are not fully committed to the vision of the church, you must either change the vision or change the deacons.

We design the Vision Statement to bring the church to, or typically, back to, the starting phase of the life cycle. Deacons should be the leaders of the congregation in adopting, and in commitment to, the vision itself. This commitment will be a motivator for the whole congregation to respond.

Deacons, along with the staff, become the pacesetters for the congregation in the fulfillment of the vision. They cannot move forward in carrying out the vision and leave the congregation behind. Neither can they expect the congregation to move forward at a pace ahead of the pastor and deacons. Good leaders establish a pace that challenges the body to move forward while being mindful that moving too rapidly will leave many unable to keep up.

Deacons must work closely with the pastor in planning for the next vision update. As the church reaches the goals outlined in the vision, the danger of becoming complacent exists. Deacons must be aware that becoming complacent opens the door to the maintenance phase of the life cycle and all that follows. As the church continues the process of living through its vision they must remain open to receiving and adopting new visions in the future.

The ideal for any church is to evaluate the work it is doing each year. This evaluation will provide an opportunity to celebrate achievements and to make course corrections as necessary. An annual review of the vision becomes a healthy method of keeping the church on track.

Writing the Vision Statement

When the local church writes and adopts their Vision Statement, under the leadership of The Holy Spirit, they choose their ultimate goals and methods employed in reaching those goals. One goal they should include in their Vision Statement is the Great Commission (Matthew 28:19-20). Properly identifying the purpose of the church and the God-inspired functions of the church will help the church fulfill The Great Commission.

Dr. James Draper, president of the Baptist Sunday School Board, states: "If churches are to grow constantly, they must perform five biblical functions. If your church only does one of the five, it is dysfunctional. Even if it follows through on four of the five, it still is not functioning fully and properly." [20] Evidently, a Vision Statement must begin with the recognition of the Great Commission as the charge to the churches and the five biblical functions as the skeleton on which we hang the plans and work of the church.

Five Biblical Functions of the Church
Evangelism

Evangelism takes place when believers share the gospel message of Jesus Christ with unbelievers. This function is the responsibility of every believer. The church establishes training programs, helps in finding those without Christ, and provides materials and encouragement to become effective witnesses. Draper says, "Evangelism is the heartbeat of the

---

[20]Dr. James Draper. *Bridges to the Future: A Challenge for Southern Baptists.* (Nashville: Convention Press, 1994), p. 45.

church." [21] The spiritual mind-set and experience of the deacon ideally provide a model for personal evangelism to the members of the body.

Discipleship

The scriptures show that new believers begin their Christian Life as newborn babies. Discipleship is the process of Christian growth in the life of new believers. The goal of every believer should be to be more like Christ in our daily walk with him. Discipleship is most effective when matured believers teach new believers about growing in God's grace. They transfer this teaching from the life of the mature believer through the process of formal training, prayer, scripture reading, and by becoming a model of the Christian lifestyle. Here again, the deacon is the best example of Christ alive in the heart of a sincere believer.

Fellowship

The local church consists of a body of believers who pledge themselves to the Lord Jesus Christ. Further, they have followed him in "believers' baptism" as an act of obedience to His teachings. Since all members in the Body of Christ enter that body in the same fashion, a local church should be consistent with the make-up of the community it serves.

In the second chapter of Acts, Luke reminds us that the body of Christ is a growing body. It should be alive and well at any point in time of its existence. The body exists for mutual support, worship, and service. To have true fellowship, each member shares in all events of life with one

---

[21]Draper. p. 45.

another. When one is rejoicing in the victories of life, the whole church rejoices. When one suffers, the whole membership feels the pain and works together to relieve its impact.

True fellowship depends upon love, forgiveness, and an attitude of sharing among all of its members as it strives to build itself up for the sake of the Lord. The fellowship serves each other mutually to express our commitment to God through worship, evangelism, and ministry. The building of relationships within the body provides a readiness to both receive and project our mutual concern.

Ministry

James Draper says, "The church that does not minister is not a church." [22] in Matthew 25:31-46, Jesus explains that a ministry expressed to our fellow man is in fact an expression of our love for Him. It also reminds us that a failure in the ministry to our fellow man in his time of need is an indication that we do not have a relationship with Jesus Himself.

Dr. Harold Graves, in his book, The Nature and Functions of a Church, deals extensively with the responsibility of the church in the area of the ministry. He states the following: "Ministry has a twofold purpose. First, it is expressing Christian love in Jesus' name. Second, ministering is the meeting the total needs of a person-spiritual and physical,

---

[22]Draper. p. 47.

individually and collectively." [23]

Graves shows that ministering to the needs of others is the responsibility of every church member. Therefore, the church has the responsibility of teaching the members the scriptural mandate for ministry and then exposing them to the needs of the community. The church must then develop the necessary programs to address the needs it has discovered. The ministry outside the church includes the next-door neighbor, but also the needs around the world.

Howse and Thomason, in their book, A Church Organized and Functioning, warns us of the possibility of growing churches becoming "insensitive to the suffering, loneliness, and physical needs of fellow members and persons in the community or around the world . . . Ministry may be expressed individually or collectively . . . congregations must learn to suffer with mankind wherever suffering takes place."[24]

Worship

We form the church, by its nature, to collectively worship our Lord. Worship takes place through praise in song, prayer, giving, obedience, and the sharing of God's Word. Worshipers should experience the presence of God, Himself, as He speaks to us in times of prayer and meditation. Draper

---

[23]Dr. Harold Graves. The Nature and Functions of a Church. (Nashville: Convention Press, (1963), p. 124.

[24]Howse and Thomason. A Church Organized and Functioning, (Nashville: Convention Press, 1963), p.14.

says, "worship is entering God's presence to hear from Him, to be moved by Him, to be transformed by Him, and to leave committed to Him."[25]

Deacons have several responsibilities in helping the congregation establish a Vision Statement and assisting in achieving those goals. They should also help the pastor while updating the Vision Statement, and in leading the congregation to understand their responsibilities in participating in the work of the church.

The deacons should be knowledgeable in all of the elements of the vision and the interpretation of the various programs of the church as they relate to the vision. The deacons become responsible for sharing the church vision to all members, new and old, and to those interested in the work of the church in their community.

---

[25]Draper, p. 49.

10

 ## Seizing the Day

Early in my ministry, I began to see the importance of deacon ministry so I spent a substantial amount of time studying its role in the church. This study convinced me that our church was undervaluing deacons' potential by relegating their role to administration. With permission of the deacon body, I began to teach what I was learning to them.

With enthusiasm, they not only allowed me to teach it, but to apply the principles I was teaching. We decided we were going to become a ministering body, learn how to share our faith, and learn how to minister to others in times of need.

We decided to follow the "family ministry plan." It is a program that divides the church families between the deacons, who in turn, minister to their needs. One new policy decision arose from this plan. Anytime someone applied for membership in the church by baptism, letter or statement of faith, I would assign them to a deacon who would visit the family before accepting them into membership. During the visit, the deacon would give the prospective member a new member's packet which included a copy of the budget, calendar and membership directory. They also explained the deacons' ministry and how they were on call to minister to their family's needs.

Charlie, the chairman of the deacons, did not like the plan because Baptist customarily accept prospective members on the spot, not at a future business meeting. I had a lot of respect for him, after all, he had served as a deacon longer than I had been alive. We discussed Charlie's objection and decided that, as an autonomous church, we could receive members as we felt best. Charlie still did not like the idea, but because the others were enthusiastic he was willing to try it.

Our policy was to assign an equal number of families to each deacon Each Sunday, during our deacons' prayer meeting, we always discussed who would receive the new people who joined the church that morning.

Our church really grew during those years. We doubled in attendance over the next four years and had very little conflict. Obviously, the deacons' leadership contributed to the health of the church.

One Sunday I found out that Charlie was beginning to support the program totally. Charlie was not the kind of guy who could say, "I was wrong in opposing this organization, I think we should move forward with it." But he did find a way to communicate the sentiment.

A family came forward to join our church. I was going through the ritual, explaining our policy for receiving new members. Then I assigned them to the appropriate deacon. While making the assignment, Charlie interrupted me and said "Now Pastor, wait just a minute, this is a fine young family that will be a tremendous asset to our church. Put them in my group. I think they ought to go in my group since I am the chairman of the deacons."

At first I was defensive, thinking Charlie was challenging

my authority. He was not due a family for a while and I knew that I was assigning them to the right deacon. Then with a big smile on his face, he apologized and said, "Pastor, I'm sorry for interrupting, but when I see a family like this coming into our church, I'm excited about it. I just think our Deacons' Family Plan is such an important part of what we do. I just wanted them in my group. I'm sorry. Assign them where they should be." It was Charlie's way of apologizing for not being fully supportive at first and saying "Pastor, it is working and it is working well."

Men like Charlie "come beside" their pastor to support the church's policies and plans for the ministry that make a plan work. It is essential that your church have a plan. It might be the one our church was following, or it might be another one, but you need a plan.

Effective organization, leadership, and planning will create a pathway to success. The deacons should construct the organizational structure of the deacon body on the foundation of the purpose statement of the church, and the purpose statement of the deacons themselves. They should design the structure as a guide to the ongoing ministry of the deacons. The structure needs to be as simply constructed as possible based on the size and function of the body.

A deacon body of six or fewer deacons could operate without dividing the leadership responsibilities. Electing a chairperson and recording secretary should suffice. The planning and carrying out the ministry would be the function of the body as a whole. Formation of committees or subgroups would create more burdens without additional benefit.

Groups of seven to fifteen might find it beneficial to select individuals with responsibilities of leadership in areas needing specific attention. Again, drawing from the purpose statement of the body, these responsibilities might include: church ordinances, training leader, assistant chairperson, recording secretary, fellowship director, and ministry leader. The functions of the leaders in each area are self explanatorily. The ministry leader would be responsible for the assignment of families to specific deacons (as in the family ministry plan), or assignments necessary to fulfill the needs of the ministry system adopted by the body and the church. In some cases, they might use a rotational method in a deacon-of-the-week plan. Others may make outreach or ministry assignments on an "as needed" basis.

Deacon bodies that are larger than sixteen would expand the role of the specific leader to form a committee within the body to do the tasks at hand. The ordinance person would become the ordinance committee and so on. The training director would become the chairman of the training committee with the inclusion of other members as needed. Additionally, they might use temporary committees as the need arises.

They should take the selection of the chairman and other leaders as a serious matter since their work may determine the success of the whole. The skills of the individual as leaders must be a real consideration. Some deacons may be good followers and good at the ministry, but weak at planning or leadership. In an attempt to be fair to all deacons, some have selected leaders based on "whose turn is it to be chairman" concept. While this may seem appropriate, it requires the deacons to risk their work on an unskilled or inadequate leader. Still others have elected persons because they are "not present to decline." Again, the whole body will feel the limitations of poor leadership and it will extend to the total church and community.

We cannot overstate the role of the pastor as leader of the deacons. The elected leadership directs the ongoing ministry of the deacons, while the pastor is responsible for the care of the flock. His responsibilities include the motivation and direction of the deacon body, his fellow team members. A pastor who neglects close ties to this body should not expect their ministry to be an integral part of the total ministry of the church. They need his guidance, direction, and supporting love as much as any group or individual in the church. Pastors must remember that deacons need ministry too.

Deacon ministries must give attention to the planning process in performance of their duties. The first consideration of planning is to select a ministry system. They can choose the system from a variety of sources, or it may be the result of self-planning by the body itself. If an existing system is selected, such as *The Deacon Family Ministry Plan*, the deacons should feel free to expand or subtract from the program, based on the specific needs of the congregation. This plan, like all others, will require at least a moderate amount of time invested in training. The deacons should not begin a system for deacon ministries until they fully understand it. The deacons and the church should be aware of the expectations for the ministry in the plan itself.

Caution: In selecting a ministry system, take into consideration the number of persons required for the system to be effective. Dividing the number of family units by ten determines the most effective number of deacons for the Family Ministry Plan in the church. The result will be the approximate number of deacons necessary to maintain the program. A church of 500 family units would need fifty active deacons participating in the program. Having fewer deacons will result in the overburdening of the active deacons. Often this will create "deacon burn out" or neglect of at least some church members. Either condition leads to a breakdown of the system. When a system fails, finding a suitable replacement is more difficult than beginning a new system.

A moderately sized church should allow a minimum of three to six months after adoption of the plan before they implement it. Each deacon should commit himself to do the duties of the plan faithfully. Both should write and approve a covenant agreement between the deacons and the church. If the system of the ministry is already in place, the formation of the covenant occurs at the installation of new deacons. If the deacons choose a system for use within the established body of deacons, they must agree upon the covenant as a group. The covenant selected or written for your church should address the function of the deacons within the system you choose.

With the ministry system in place, covenants written, and the training needs fulfilled, the deacons and church are approaching readiness for implementation. Planning a special recognition service for informing the congregation of the new ministry system initiated by the deacons is appropriate.

The purpose for adopting a ministry system is not to replace the ministry of the deacons, it is to allow the deacons to be more effective in carrying out the task that is already theirs. To some, it may seem that the cautions or concerns outweigh the benefits of the system selected. It is true that they must consider details of the program. It is also true that having such a system in place can carry the effectiveness of deacon ministries to new heights. Not only does this provide a great benefit to the church, it also raises the personal satisfaction level of the deacon.

The Soda Crate

Deacon Tom Hall is one of the finest men I ever served beside. He had a heart for ministry and was always looking for a way to minister to his families. Several years after I left his church, Tom wanted to take the Seniors of the church on a shopping trip during the middle of December. He asked his pastor if he could borrow the church's van, and he recruited members of the Youth Group to be their companions for the day to help them in any way they needed. Tom gassed up the van and was ready to drive to the first home when he noticed a faded, worn, old wooden soda crate by the side of the church. He threw it in the van at the last minute, and drove off.

At their first stop, an elderly woman was at the front door waiting for them. She had on a large coat that swallowed her small frame, and a small, dark-blue pillbox hat with a black veil. She carried a black leather purse and an ornate, carved cane with a golden tip. Smiling brightly, eyes sparkling, a male Youth escorted her to the van. Tom jumped out of the driver's seat, grabbed the soda crate, and placed it on the curb. She gave him a look he will never forget as she proudly stepped on that old crate, and with minimal assistance from anyone, she sprang through the van door and sat down. The scene repeated itself until the van was full, and they arrived at the mall.

Literally arm-in-arm, the Senior citizens and their escorts ventured into the bustling mall. The Youth were to carry the packages, assist in the monetary transactions, make sure their partners received the correct change, and take their respective Seniors to lunch. Of course some Youth took on this assignment very grudgingly, but by the time lunch was over, the openness, humor, and thankfulness of these loving Seniors completely captivated the Youth. They formed bonds that lasted long after the holidays! Their eyes reflected an overwhelming expression of God's love as the pairs walked arm-in-arm, laughing, talking, and sharing.

At 4:00, these odd-looking pairs emerged through the large glass doors of the mall. Tom had doubts about how this adventure would turn out, but when he saw the excitement and the enthusiasm of both the Teenagers and the Seniors--carrying and dropping packages, laughing and stumbling--all his doubts quickly vanished. As each Senior stepped onto the soda crate to enter the van, Tom heard numerous stories about the adventures of the day. It seemed that everyone was talking at the same time as they began the short trip back to their homes. In the rearview mirror, Tom could see whatever walls existed between those age groups crumble.

When Tom talks about that moment, he says, "I was so thankful to be a deacon. I silently thanked God for allowing me to serve Him, allowing me to serve people, and to be a catalyst in bringing God's people together."

As they arrived at the last house, the lady with the blue pillbox hat and the ornate cane gathered her packages and grasped the hand of her youth. She thanked him for being "such a gentleman" and promised to tell him more stories later. She also promised him chocolate chip cookies the next Sunday.

Tom pulled the van in front of her house and ran around to open the side door. He placed the soda crate on the curb, and took her one hand as the Youth took the other. She turned to the young Teen, thanked him again, then faced Tom. Her eyes glistening with tears of gratitude, she firmly grasped his hand. Almost silently, she said "Thank you." Those two words affirmed Tom's deacon ministry. She took a few steps toward her front door, and supported by that ornate cane, turned to Tom, winked, and said, "By the way, thank you, too, for the soda crate."

Acknowledgments

This book is made possible by a variety of contributors. Dr. Jim Wilson came along as writer/contributor and editor. Manuscript help came from several sources including:

Tim Wilson   Connie Clair
Rita Robertson   Virginia Smith
Edna McGuffin   Stephen Faupel
Barbara Weaver   Cecilia Matamoros

and others

Inspiration helps came primarily from the deacons and wives of Hillcrest Baptist Church of Vallejo, 1974-1989.

Gary & Janet Cowan   Richard & Joyce Lindsey
Charlie (dec.) & Lucy Jones   Dan (dec.) & Mildred Connell
Jim (dec.) & Mary Tapd   Tom & Sue Hall
Dan & Anne Turner   George & Suzi Hall
Floyd & Leona Carr   Dave & Laurel Wright

and others

Personal encouragement came from a variety of sources; including but not exclusively:

The members of First Baptist of Beverly Hills
Greg Sumii - Fermin Whittaker CSBC
Dr. Henry Webb - Dr. John Shouse
Bobbie Turner
&
The lovely Mrs. Riette Stringfellow